NORMIEVILLE: The Normie Masque

Book Illustrations 2025 by Harry Aveira

ISBN: 979-8-9990465-0-5 (Paperback) 979-8-9990465-1-2 (E-book)

Made in USA

First English edition published in the USA in 2025
Printed in the United States of America

Dear Normies and Truthers Alike,

This book comes straight from our hearts to yours, in what we know to be The Great Awakening of humanity. Our hearts ached as we watched the world stumble through 2020's "plandemic" but through God's gentle grace, our eyes were opened. We've created *Normieville: The Normie Masque*, in hopes it will light a fire, spark a story inside of you, and inspire you to share your personal stories and perspectives during one of the most challenging times the world has ever witnessed. Your voice and your personal journey will help unite us all and ensure that the world never falls for such a masquerade again. So turn the page, chuckle at the absurdity, and let your heart join ours in The Great Awakening of humanity.

With all our love, Kolette and Melissa

And you will know the truth, and the truth will set you free.
John 8:32

In the middle of the country sits a town on a hill. It's filled with countless people. The town is Normieville.

Normieville is growing. It has plans to be S.M.A.R.T.
There are cameras everywhere to tell the Normies apart.

The Normies obey and follow the rules.
The selected officials tell them how to run
the hospitals and schools.

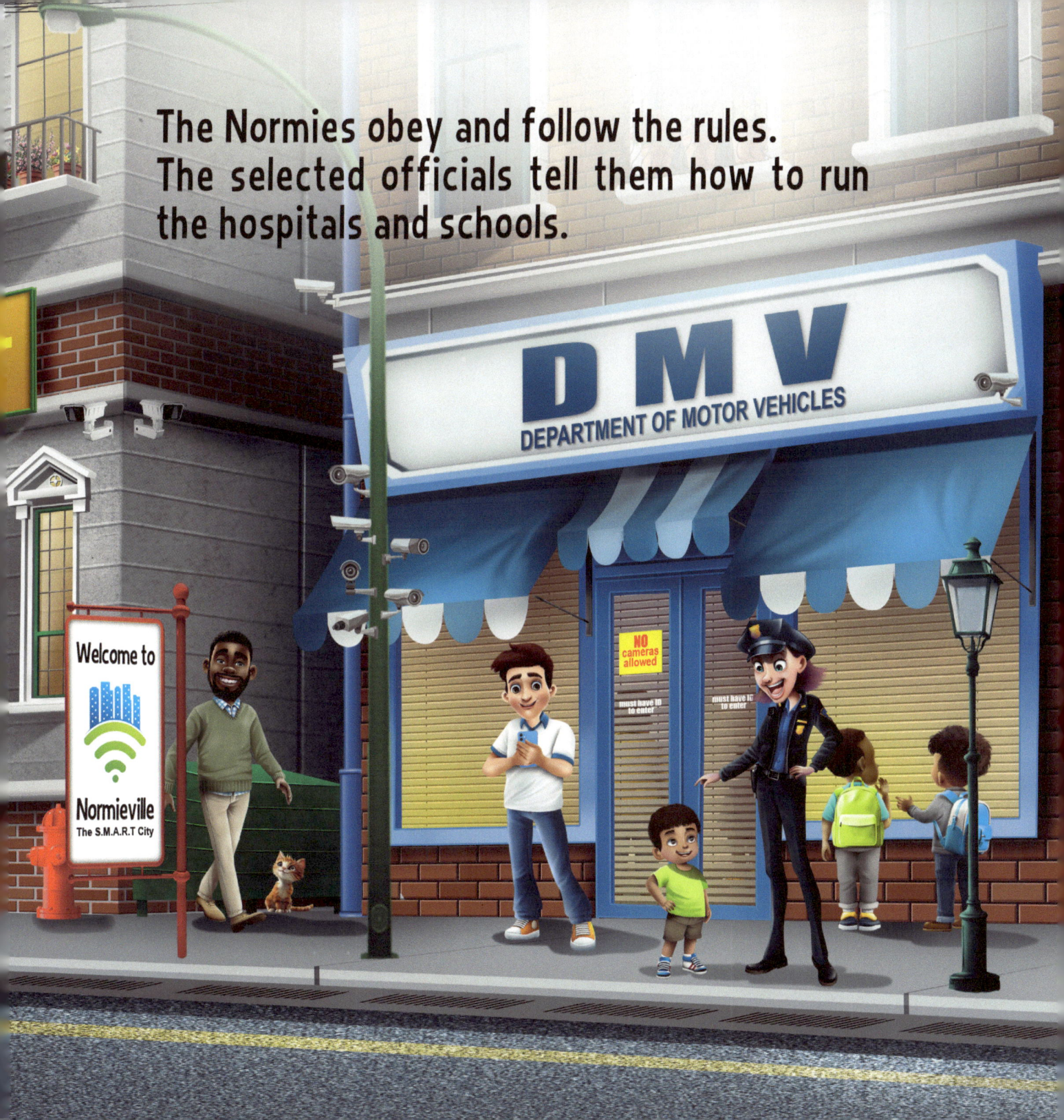

But one normie day, a scary virus came to town.
It spread like fire. And traveled all around.

The TV said "Stay at home! Don't go out!"
The Normies obeyed and fear spread throughout.

The selected officials, who said they were smart, told the Normieville people "we need a fresh restart!"

We need to have some rules to keep us all protected.
You have to wear a mask so YOU don't get infected.

Wear a mask.   **Stand 6 feet apart.**

It's all for the best. It's just a restart.

You should get it or else (that's the way we get paid).
And if you don't comply, you should all be afraid.

Afraid to lose your job, your business and friends.
Just do what you're told and then this all ends.

The Normies lined up to get a jab in the arm.
They didn't care to ask if it caused any harm.

Follow the plan, and if you do your part,
the TV said they were safe and they were smart.

The Normies obeyed and boasted online.
They posted "I'm vaccinated" on their profile design.

Wearing their masks while bragging about the shot, the Normies didn't question if it really worked or not.

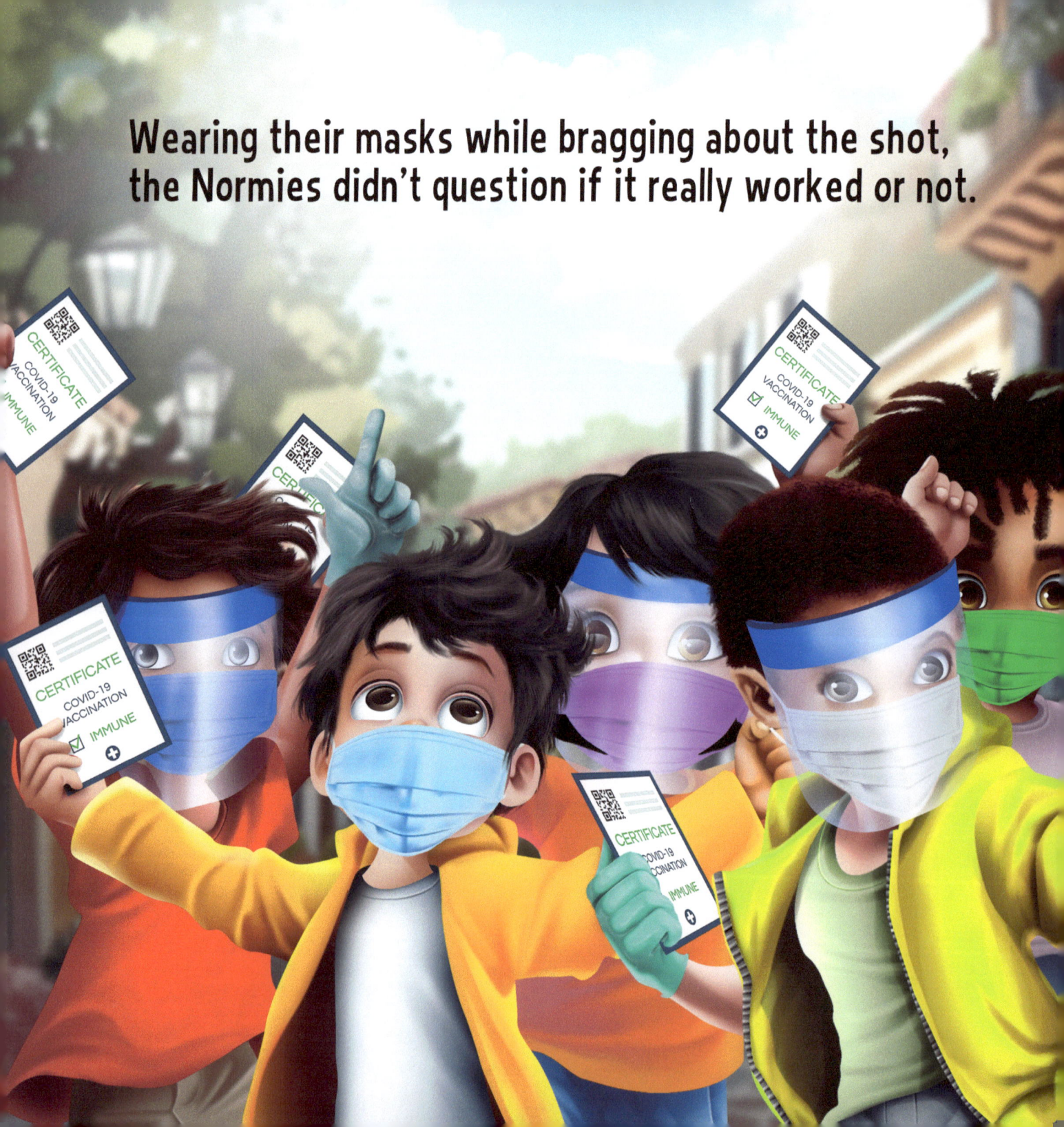

But off to the side stood a handful of people. Who didn't like what they saw and refused to be sheeple.

They stood up with courage and spoke what was true.

The Truthers stood their ground and were always attacked.

Someday the Normies will see the deceit.
They'll come to learn, they were used by the elite.

And when they do, they'll demand to have answers. They'll reach out to Truthers they once rejected and slandered.

The Truthers will be there, ready to unite.
Supporting the people and doing what is right.

www.ingramcontent.com/pod-product-compliance
Lightning Source LLC
Chambersburg PA
CBHW041720240626
47171CB00002B/14